# NO FRIENDS WITH ZERO MONEY

## YOU ARE ONLY SOLDIER FOR FIGHTING THE BATTLE OF LIFE

## S. SINGH

Copyright © S. Singh
All Rights Reserved.

I dedicate this book to those people who have a mountain of problems but have the passion to break them.

# Contents

# About Author

S. Singh is a prolific writer in English language.His another book in motivation category is " Struggle To Success Life". He is writing since 2009 for college magazine and fiction & nonfiction books in English language.His speciality is that he use common spoken language in their writing so it can understand easily and connect with reader.

# Acknowledgements

I am very grateful to my mother, Mrs. Narvada Devi who has given me a great inspiration in bringing this book to the ground. Thank you very much for this partnership.And thanks to Notion Press who provided such a platform so that I can reach this inspiration to the people.

Most grateful to my readers who have given so much love and encouragement which inspires me to write more.

# Preface

Today we are in the age of artificial intelligence and space, we have all the facilities. People are eating food in expensive restaurants, traveling the world, using branded goods.But there is also a large section which is fighting for its existence.He has access to this digital world but he does not earn enough to stand equal to this world.His problems have suppressed him so much that his thinking forced him to stay there.It is absolutely true that he came out of his illusion by making a way over your problems and you can go ahead of this world.

For this, instead of facing your problem, make it your purpose.No one's support is needed in this, you are enough. There will be difficulties, no one will support us, but we have to find the means by which these problems can be ended.

# ONE

## PROBLEMS ARE YOUR PURPOSE

Today we live in a world where Metro, Malls, World Class Restaurants, Smart

Gadgets, Digital and Easy Payment Systems, Big Companies, everything

around us. In same world there is also a world of people who have digital

gadgets and digital payment systems, many bank account in every way but

who are living on zero balance.Their problem is that they cannot tell their

problem to anyone because people do not believe it that they don't even have

100 rupees.The reason for this is that they earn only enough to pay the

installments of life.Salary credit enough so that he can only give to those from

whom he had borrowed, and can feed his dependents a little.Now again

borrowing money from the same person and then giving it

to him, this cycle
has been going on.And because of this zero balance, his friends keep distance
from him.
All this is a little normal to hear or read, but nothing is more painful than this.
These people come in such category, neither they can sell goods by handcart
nor they can do labour works.but the situation is worse than them.
I still remember when a few years ago I was living the same life.And then I
came to know that this zero balance is the biggest curse of our life when I
gave the resign from the company before the salary came.The next day
Human Resources called and told that your salary is on hold for 90 days.I
stopped breathing for a moment.My eyes filled with tears, It was feeling like
someone has sunk me deep in the water and put a big stone on it which I
cannot lift.Because at that moment 50 rupees in my pocket and even if all the
bank accounts of my family are searched, I do not get more than 10
rupees.And my mother was waiting for my salary that when the month ends,
as salary comes, she has little money in her hand to buy some ration to the house after returning it from whom she had borrowed.I did not have the courage at that time to tell the
family that salary is not going to come this month.Tears

kept falling from my

eyes all day long. I could not understand how the family would live and how

would I live without money in such a big city.And where were the friends left,

whatever they were, they either did not reply after seeing the message or did

not see it.

I had a mountain of troubles in front of me,My laptop was damaged which

required minimum 1500 to repair. My biggest problem was this, because it

was such a thing which was mandatory to join the next job.My concern was If

I don't get it on asking for 100 rupees, then how can I get 1500 rupees?

The second big problem is how a month will be spent without money, how

will I pay the rent of the room, how will I give the ration bill, how will the

rent for commuting be done. Everything that could have happened in that

time, I had, sadness, despair, pain, fear, loneliness, unemployment.I was so

upset that once upon a time it seemed better to die.

There were so many problems that I could not understand how to think? At

that time, even the beggars on the road were better than me. Tears couldn't stop coming from my eyes.At that time I came to know that no

one has more power and motivation than tears.If you are in a big problem

and you can't understand anything and feel like crying then

cry, your tears
will 100% show you the way or the spirit to fight it.
Crying!! I asked myself what is my biggest problem that made me cry?
Money. Yes or not
In that moment I vowed to myself that such a day will never come as long as I
am alive.
And Money became the biggest purpose of my life.That day and today, any
problem could not demotivate me.Apart from this, I could not see anything.

**"Nothing can be bigger than the problem which brings tears to the eyes of a
brave man."**

No matter how big the problem is, when you do not become your purpose,
then you cannot win from that problem.
Write it on a paper and paste on place where you live .

**"Make your biggest problem as your goal. You will never have to cry again in life
because of that problem."**

# TWO

# DON'T FORGET YOUR PROBLEMS

Problem always makes us cry because we forget it as soon as we get a little
comfort.
When the problem comes, we think that I will finish it and we forget our vow
slowly.We forget our own and our family's pain, we forget the tears that are
your mother's eyes, which do not let her live in peace day and night.
If we want to eliminate any problem from the root, then we have to
remember it every day, we have to remember that pain till the pain is not
exhausted.
That fire is burning in your heart, it should always keep burning till that
problem is burnt to ashes.Do whatever you have to do for this, even if you
make a pamphlet and put it everywhere, wherever you live,

where you

work.Don't give yourself rest because your problem is looking for

opportunity.Work beyond your capabilities because you don't have to rise

above average. You have to rise above zero.You don't have to see the level of

people, you have to see your zero, because of your zero no one is with you.

And you can do that work with stubbornness and passion only when you

remember your pain.

**" *Always remember that you are at zero now.* "**

# THREE
## END OF HELP

There will come a time when no one will be with you, you will be living alone.

You will go to everyone, everyone will ignore you. There will be little help,

yet people will refuse to help. Our world is like this, money goes to those who

have it. You must have seen, the bank gives credit cards, loans to those who

have money and they do not even need it. People want to help only those

who can help them.

It is human nature that when we are in some problem, we ask for help from

someone from whom they hope. We curse them if we don't get help. They are

riff – raff, I'll show them when the time comes.

Why?

Is this their problem or is it created because of them??

No.

It's not their problem, it's my problem, so they're not responsible for that. So

if they do not help us, it is their choice, if we feel bad, then we have to do this
in our life that we do not have to ask for their help. Think, are we born to
beg? In the same organization, a person is earning so much, who is coming
daily in expensive vehicles, eating well in restaurants, wearing good clothes.
And there is one of us who do not have our own car, do not have very
expensive clothes and accessories, are not eating well, yet we are like this.

Because where do we have time, by crying and cursing others that people are
not helping me. You have convinced yourself that you are poor. From the day
you break this perception, you will not take time to eliminate that difference.
Swear today I have to delete this word from my life" I need a help"
As there is a saying here, **God also helps those who are capable of helping themselves.**

# FOUR

## RIGHT SURFACE

If you ask someone where do you get gold?

The answer will be inside the earth. Isn't it?

Will we get gold anywhere if we start digging?

No.

Gold will be found only on the surface under which it originated.And if we

explore that surface, then dig it, then only we can mine gold.

Similarly, we wouldn't get everywhere the gold we want, for that we have to

explore a right surface, only then we will get the benefit of the hard work we

are doing.Sometimes we try too hard but things don't happen according to

us.Because that's not our right surface.Put more of your effort into exploring the right surface.Find such a way that even if you stuck somewhere, the resources keep coming to you.Always remember this,

**"If you don't find a way to make money while you sleep, you will work untill you die."**

Sometimes it takes a long time to get this right surface but eventually we
have to get that right surface. You will get the value of your hard work as soon
as you come to the right place. Your problems will slowly start leaving you
like those friends who left you because of your money.

# Task Assign For You

1. Write down your biggest problem.
    2.What is your right surface ?